JAMES TAYLOR
COMPLETE
VOLUME ONE

Front Cover Photography: Lynn Goldsmith

CONTENTS

JAMES TAYLOR

JAMES TAYLOR

CAROLINA IN MY MIND

Words and Music by
JAMES TAYLOR

In my mind, __ I'm gone to Car - o - li - na.

Can't you see the sun - shine? Can't you just feel the moon __ shin - ing?

DON'T TALK NOW

Words and Music by
JAMES TAYLOR and ZACHARY WIESNER

BRIGHTEN YOUR NIGHT WITH MY DAY

Words and Music by
JAMES TAYLOR

TAKING IT IN

Words and Music by
JAMES TAYLOR

KNOCKING 'ROUND THE ZOO

Words and Music by
JAMES TAYLOR

28

THE BLUES IS JUST A BAD DREAM

Words and Music by
JAMES TAYLOR

3. My mind is rambling
   It's just like some rolling stone
   Since that nightmare's come to stay
   My thoughts just don't belong
   They say the blues is just a bad dream
   They say it lives inside your head
   But when it's lonely in the morning
   You're bound to wish that you were dead.

SUNSHINE, SUNSHINE

Words and Music by
JAMES TAYLOR

2. Rising too late to chase the cold,
   failing to change the frost-bitten dew,
She's trading her mood of yellow gold,
   for frost-bitten shades of silver blue.
Friends and lovers, past and gone,
   and no one waiting further on;
I'm running short of things to be,
   and sunshine means a lot to me.
Sunshine, oh, sunshine.

SOMETHING'S WRONG

Words and Music by
JAMES TAYLOR

SOMETHING IN THE WAY SHE MOVES

Words and Music by
JAMES TAYLOR

NIGHT OWL

Words and Music by
JAMES TAYLOR

JAMES TAYLOR
SWEET BABY JAMES

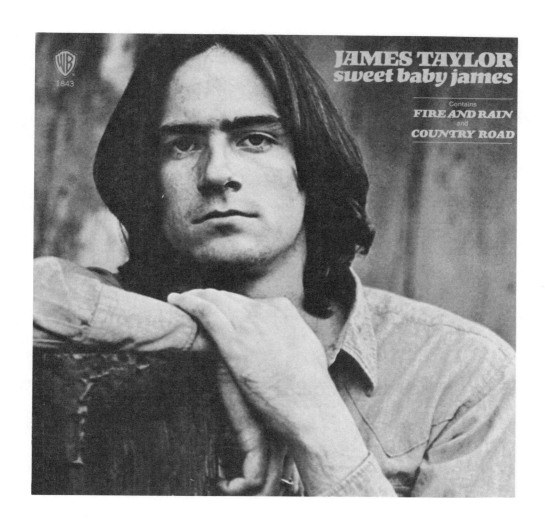

SWEET BABY JAMES

Words and Music by
JAMES TAYLOR

LO AND BEHOLD

Words and Music by
JAMES TAYLOR

SUNNY SKIES

Words and Music by
JAMES TAYLOR

COUNTRY ROAD

Words and Music by
JAMES TAYLOR

Take to the high - way. Won't you lend me your name?
Sail on home to Je - sus, won't you, good girls and boys?

Your way and my way seem to be one and the same.
I'm all in piec - es. You can have your own choice. But

Ma - ma don't un - der - stand it. She wants to know where I've been.
I can see a heav - en - ly band full of an - gels and they're com - ing to set me free.

* Guitarists: Tune sixth string down to D.

STEAMROLLER

Words and Music by
JAMES TAYLOR

2. Well, I'm a cement mixer; a churning urn of burning funk.
   Yes, I'm a cement mixer for you, babe; a churning urn of burning funk.
   Well, I'm a demolition derby, yeah; a hefty hunk of steaming junk.

3. Now, I'm a napalm bomb, babe, just guaranteed to blow your mind.
   Yeah, I'm a napalm bomb for you, baby, just guaranteed to blow your mind.
   And if I can't have your love for my own, now, sweet child, won't be nothing left behind.
   It seems how lately, babe, got a bad case of steamroller blues.

ANYWHERE LIKE HEAVEN

Words and Music by
JAMES TAYLOR

OH BABY DON'T LOOSE YOUR LIP ON ME

Words and Music by
JAMES TAYLOR

SUITE FOR 20G

Words and Music by
JAMES TAYLOR

Slip-ping a - way_ what can _ I say_ Won't you stay _ in - side my month _ of May_ And hold on to _ me, gold - en day,_ slip-ping a - way._

Sun - shine _ on _ my wall to

76

BLOSSOM

Words and Music by
JAMES TAYLOR

FIRE AND RAIN

Words and Music by
JAMES TAYLOR

see you, ba - by, one more time __ a - gain, __ now.

Thought I'd see __ you one more time __ a - gain. __

There's just a few things com - ing my way this time a - round. __

Repeat and fade

JAMES TAYLOR

MUD SLIDE SLIM

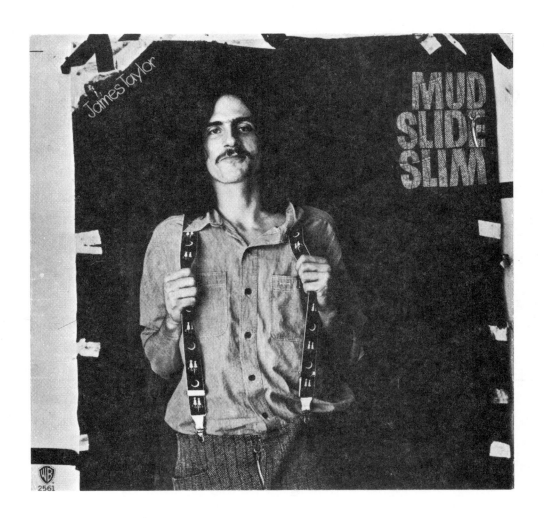

LOVE HAS BROUGHT ME AROUND

Words and Music by
JAMES TAYLOR

Love has brought me a-round. Love has brought me a-round, yes, it has.

Love has brought me a-round. Love has brought me a-round.

When my Now I know you know

what I've got to say is an old cli - ché

YOU'VE GOT A FRIEND

Words and Music by
CAROLE KING

PLACES IN MY PAST

Words and Music by
JAMES TAYLOR

RIDING ON A RAILROAD

Words and Music by
JAMES TAYLOR

MUD SLIDE SLIM

Words and Music by
JAMES TAYLOR

SOLDIERS

Words and Music by
JAMES TAYLOR

ISN'T IT NICE TO BE HOME AGAIN

Words and Music by
JAMES TAYLOR

Late last night,_ so far _ a - way, I dreamed my- self a dream._

Well, I dreamed _ I was _ so all _ a - lone.

Is - n't it nice _ to be home a - gain?_ I said,

HEY MISTER, THAT'S ME UP ON THE JUKEBOX

Words and Music by
JAMES TAYLOR

Hey, mis-ter, that's me up _ on _ the juke-box. _

I'm the one that's sing-in' this _ sad song. _

Well, I'll cry ev-'ry time that you slip in one _ more dime _ and

let the boy sing the sad _ one one _ more _ time. _

YOU CAN CLOSE YOUR EYES

Words and Music by
JAMES TAYLOR

LONG AGO AND FAR AWAY

Words and Music by
JAMES TAYLOR

LET ME RIDE

**Words and Music by
JAMES TAYLOR**

Hand me down __ my gold - en crown __ and let __ me ride. __

Don't de - ny __ the high - way in __ my soul. __

Jump and sing __ that sil - ver thing __ that I feel __ in - side _____ me.

HIGHWAY SONG

Words and Music by
JAMES TAYLOR

JAMES TAYLOR
ONE MAN DOG

NOBODY BUT YOU

Words and Music by
JAMES TAYLOR

ONE MAN PARADE

Words and Music by
JAMES TAYLOR

Moderately

Do be-lieve I'm gon-na clap my hands,_ I think_ I might tap my feet,_

put to-geth-er a one-man band,_ take it walk-

-in' on down_ the street,_ Have a one-man_____ pa-rade,_

* Thumb optional

CHILI DOG

Words and Music by
JAMES TAYLOR

FOOL FOR YOU

Words and Music by
JAMES TAYLOR

Moderately

My la-dy don't al-low____ the life I lead,

She don't a-bide by some of the com-pa-ny that I keep,

She takes oc-ca-sion to crit-i-cize____ and car-ry on.____

I love her so____ I just can't stand it no more,____ I'm a fool

she jumps at the chance to tease me with her bod - y.

B7   C   A   Am7/D

Lord, I love that thing so, just can't stand it no more. I'm a

Gm7/C   F/G

fool for you babe, sure am, I'm a fool for you babe.

Repeat and fade

8va bassa

NEW TUNE

Words and Music by
JAMES TAYLOR

INSTRUMENTAL 1

Music by
JAMES TAYLOR

BACK ON THE STREET AGAIN

Words and Music by
DANIEL KORTCHMAR

DON'T LET ME BE LONELY TONIGHT

Words and Music by
JAMES TAYLOR

WOH, DON'T YOU KNOW

Words and Music by
JAMES TAYLOR, DANIEL KORTCHMAR,
and LELAND SKLAR

Lis-ten here now, don't— you come round talk - in' 'bout o - ver yon - der, —

Bound to wake up the walk - in' man— in me and I'm bound to wan - der.

Talk - in' all a - bout Spoon - y Lee Blue - bones, look - in' just like Sher - lock Holmes. —

Search - in' for a nee-dle in a hay-stack, see him eat - in' lots of fat back bass,

INSTRUMENTAL II

Music by
JAMES TAYLOR

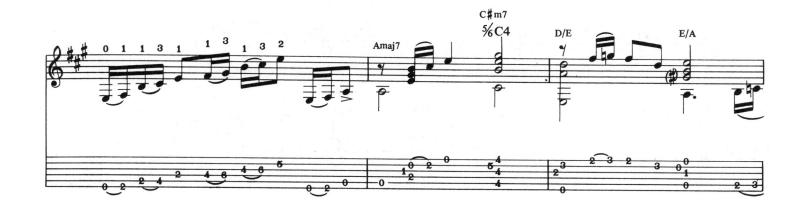

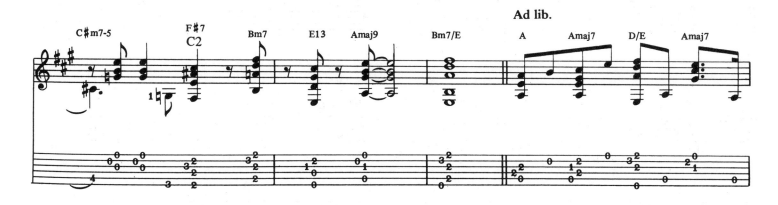

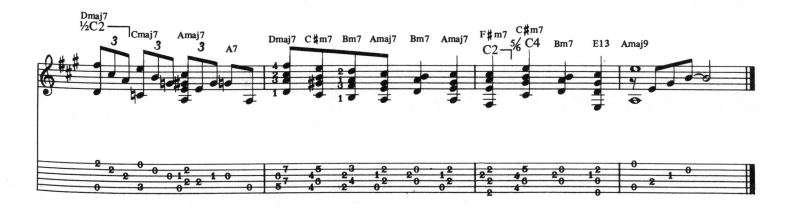

ONE MORNING IN MAY

Words and Music by
JAMES TAYLOR

HYMN

Words and Music by
JAMES TAYLOR

FANFARE

Words and Music by
JAMES TAYLOR

Briskly

Hard Rock (♩ = ♪)

Some-one turned the time on, ___ an-oth-er day is dead and gone, ___ a

life-time is slip-pin' ___ a-way, ___ babe. ___

LITTLE DAVID

Words and Music by
JAMES TAYLOR

MESCALITO

Words and Music by
JAMES TAYLOR

JIG

Music by
JAMES TAYLOR

DANCE

Words and Music by
JAMES TAYLOR

Come on, ba - by, while the moon is high, pick up your heels and dance. _

Don't be ner - vous and don't be shy, _ and give your - self a chance. _ You can

dance, Pick up your shoes and lose your blues, pick 'em up, Lord, put 'em back down and a-

round and a-round and a-round and a-round. Come on, babe, it must be fun _ to be

No - bod - y here to-night came to look at you no, _____ no, no. Well, I

bet you five dol - lars that some - bod - y starts a fire back in the woods. Hey, now

D.S. 𝄋 *al Coda* Coda

ev -'ry-bod-y here to-night _ came to boo -gie, have a good time, too._

But if I could lose my mind, if I could throw my-self_ a - way.

holding back

JAMES TAYLOR
WALKING MAN

ROCK 'N' ROLL IS MUSIC NOW

Words and Music by
JAMES TAYLOR

WALKING MAN

Words and Music by
JAMES TAYLOR

Moving in silent desperation,

keeping an eye on the Holy Land.

208

grow, no, ___ so he don't hoe_ the row___ for no one.

Coda

but not the walk-ing man.

Repeat and fade (vocal ad lib)

Repeat and fade

Vocal Ad Lib

He's the walking man, born to walk,
Walk on, walking man.
Well now, would he have wings to fly,
Would he be free?
Golden wings against the sky.
Walking man, walk on by,
So long, walking man, so long.

ME AND MY GUITAR

Words and Music by
JAMES TAYLOR

Vocal Ad Lib

Oh, maybe a few friends fall by for tea,
A little bit of who do you love.
But pay no attention to the man behind the curtain,
It's me and my guitar.
Having fun, boogie, woogie, uh-huh,
Me and my guitar.

LET IT ALL FALL DOWN

Words and Music by
JAMES TAYLOR

DADDY'S BABY

Words and Music by
JAMES TAYLOR

Lyrics:
Dad-dy's ba - by, what's got you think - ing, what's got you sink - ing so low?___ Is there

MIGRATION

Words and Music by
JAMES TAYLOR

Moderately slow, in 2

No chord

Dis-tant hands in for-eign lands__ are turn-ing__ hid-den wheels,__

caus-ing things to come a-bout__ which no one seems to feel.__ All in-

D/E   A/E   Asus4/E   E

vis-i-ble from where we stand,__ the con-nec-tions come to pass, and

though too strange to com-pre-hend, they af - fect us none - the - less, yes.___

Once a - gain___ a time___

___ of change; ___ oh, the change makes mu -

sic, and the chil- dren will dance.___

HELLO OLD FRIEND

Words and Music by
JAMES TAYLOR

FADING AWAY

Words and Music by
JAMES TAYLOR

JAMES TAYLOR

GORILLA

MEXICO

Words and Music by
JAMES TAYLOR

GORILLA

Words and Music by
JAMES TAYLOR

MUSIC

Words and Music by
JAMES TAYLOR

Turn on the mu - sic, strike up the mu - sic,
Crank out the mu - sic, give me mu - sic,
Give me mu - sic, Mis - ter Mu - sic,

let the mu-sic change my mind.
let the mu-sic fill the air.
let the mu-sic be there

My dear friend, your head's been sink-ing like a stone. You must try think-ing like a

cloud some-time. Just leave a hap-py side out loud some-time. There's a

HOW SWEET IT IS (TO BE LOVED BY YOU)

Words and Music by
EDDIE HOLLAND, LAMONT DOZIER
and BRIAN HOLLAND

258

WANDERING

Traditional — Musical Adaptation and Additional Lyrics by
JAMES TAYLOR

I've been wan-d'rin' ear-ly and late, from New York Cit-y to the Gold-en Gate.
been in the ar-my, I've worked on a farm, and all I've got to show is the mus-cle in my arm. And it
Snakes in the o-cean, eels in the sea, I let a red-head-ed wom-an make a fool out of me.

I WAS A FOOL TO CARE

Words and Music by
JAMES TAYLOR

YOU MAKE IT EASY

Words and Music by
JAMES TAYLOR

LIGHTHOUSE

Words and Music by
JAMES TAYLOR

ANGRY BLUES

Words and Music by
JAMES TAYLOR

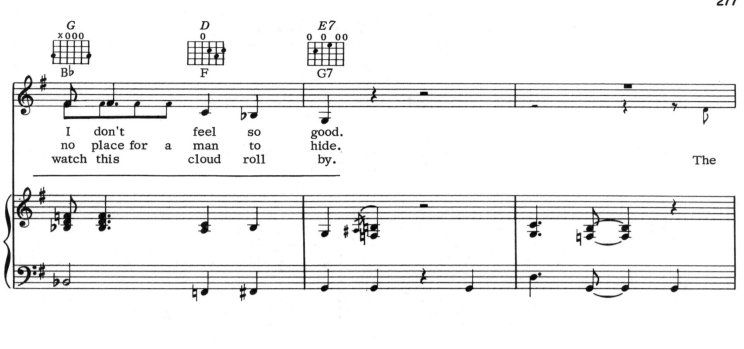

I don't feel so good.
no place for a man to hide.
watch this cloud roll by. The

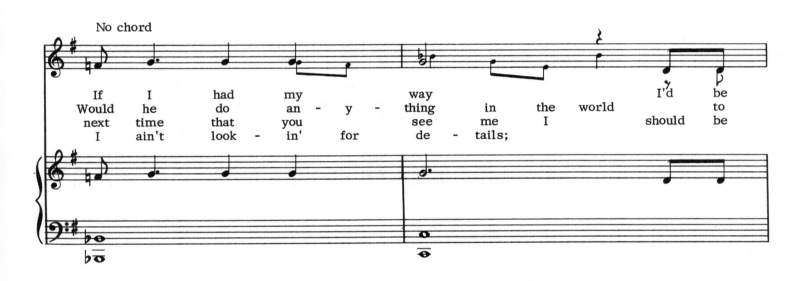

No chord

If I had my way I'd be
Would he do an - y - thing in the world to
next time do that you see me I should be
I ain't look - in' for de - tails;

sit - ting on top of ___ the world. But
make him feel bet - ter ___ in - side? When the
shin - ing like the Fourth of ___ Ju - ly. Gon - na
won't you just give me ___ a clue.

SARAH MARIA

Words and Music by
JAMES TAYLOR

280

LOVE SONGS

Words and Music by
JAMES TAYLOR